# Rescuing Rialto

## A Baby Sea Otter's Story

# Rescuing Rialto

## A Baby Sea Otter's Story

Words by **Lynda V. Mapes**

Photographs by **Alan Berner**

**ROARING BROOK PRESS**
New York

For all the animals, and the people who love them —L.V.M.

For those who rescued, cared for, and brought Rialto
to a safe and secure place —A.B.

Copyright © 2019 by *The Seattle Times*

Published by Roaring Brook Press
Roaring Brook Press is a division of Holtzbrinck
Publishing Holdings Limited Partnership
175 Fifth Avenue, New York, NY 10010

mackids.com

All rights reserved

Library of Congress Control Number: 2017957299
ISBN 978-1-250-14764-6

Our books may be purchased in bulk for promotional,
educational, or business use. Please contact your local
bookseller or the Macmillan Corporate and Premium Sales
Department at (800) 221-7945 ext. 5442 or by email at
MacmillanSpecialMarkets@macmillan.com.

First edition, 2019
Additional photographs: Pages 5 and 7 by Joseph R. Alcorn,
National Park Service
Page 6 by Curved Light USA/Alamy Stock Photo
Pages 8, 24–26 by Tom and Pat Leeson/Leeson Photo
Page 31 by Frans Lanting Studio/Alamy Stock Photo
Illustration by Cathy Bobak
Printed in China by Hung Hing Off-set Printing Co. Ltd.,
Heshan City, Guangdong Province
10  9  8  7  6  5  4  3  2  1

**Opposite page:** Rialto looked like a wet, sandy towel washed up on the beach.

**T**HE BABY SEA OTTER was hungry. And he was all alone. Where had his mother gone? He cried and cried. Normally, a baby sea otter would never be separated from its mother for long. But something had gone wrong.

He was washed up and stranded on Rialto Beach at Olympic National Park in northern Washington state.

Rialto Beach at Olympic National Park is so wild that it was a wonder the baby sea otter was found at all.

Visitors to the beach that sunny morning of the first day in August saw that the baby sea otter was in distress. They alerted a park ranger. When he arrived, Joe Alcorn saw what looked like a crumpled, sandy old towel. Except it was moving. And shrieking.

Waves crashed over the baby sea otter. He kept trying to crawl back to the water, and to his mother. But each time, a powerful wave would send him tumbling over and over again, shoving him roughly back on the sand. The baby otter was barely strong enough to right himself. He didn't have much time left.

Joe called the Washington Sea Otter Stranding Network. One of the network's volunteers, Dyanna Lambourn, set out for the beach right away.

When she arrived, she heard the baby otter shrieking from far away. "Eeeee! Eeeee!" Baby otters have very loud voices so their mothers can hear them over the wind and waves. Then Dyanna saw him. What should she do?

If she picked him up, the pup would become used to humans and would never be able to go back to the wild. But if she left him, he would surely die. By that time it was early evening, and the pup had been out there alone all day—maybe even longer. Dyanna called people she worked with at the U.S. Fish and Wildlife Service. Sea otters are protected by law, and Dyanna needed help deciding what to do. After speaking with them, she leaned over and picked up the pup.

She settled him in a plastic tote in her car and started driving. The next challenge was finding a veterinarian or aquarium to help. Each time Dyanna made a phone call, the pup would scream. He shrieked and shrieked. Finally, the Seattle Aquarium said it would help. Dyanna hurried to Seattle.

Rialto was exhausted, and each wave sent him tumbling over and over.

No one knows how Rialto became separated from his mother. In the wild, only an accident of some kind separates a mother sea otter from her pup.

What is the thickest, softest thing you can think of? Now think of something thicker, softer, and fuzzier. Add big brown eyes. A warm, wriggly body under all that fur. Velvety soft paws.

Now imagine all sorts of sounds: soft coos, small squeaks, tiny groans. That's Rialto, a baby northern sea otter named for the beach where he was found.

Baby sea otters are helpless. They can float. They are born with their eyes open. But they can't swim, groom, or feed themselves. So a baby sea otter never leaves its mother. The baby sleeps on her chest or nurses on her tummy, between her paws, as she floats on her back in the ocean. She will loop kelp around the pup to secure him when she dives down in the water to get food. That's to keep her pup from drifting away while she's gone.

There are lots of animals that would love to eat a baby otter, such as eagles. In Alaska, brown bears, killer whales, and wolves prey on them. Baby sea otters, including those in their mother's care, have only a fifty percent chance of survival in the wild.

A pup that washed up on the beach like Rialto had would not live long without his mother to feed him, fluff his fur, and keep him clean and warm and safe. Even after he was rescued, it was not certain that Rialto would survive.

It was almost midnight by the time Dyanna and Rialto arrived at the Seattle Aquarium. Sea otter specialist Shawn Larson was waiting for them, and she knew just what to do. She had raised baby sea otters at the aquarium before.

Shawn knew Rialto was hungry. Like a human baby, he needed lots of nutrients. So she made him formula using puppy milk replacement powder, warm water, and clams, mixing it all up in a blender and putting it in a baby's bottle.

"Are you ready, Muffin?" she asked, and then gave Rialto his first bottle. She got towels—lots and *lots* of warm towels—to get Rialto fluffed up, clean, warm, and dry.

The staff at the Seattle Aquarium stayed with the baby otter every minute. He was never alone. Someone stayed with him all night. Someone was there the next morning when he woke up. Even on the weekends, when most people went home, one of Rialto's caregivers stayed with him. It took a rotating staff of about twenty people just to do what Rialto's mother would have done for him in the wild.

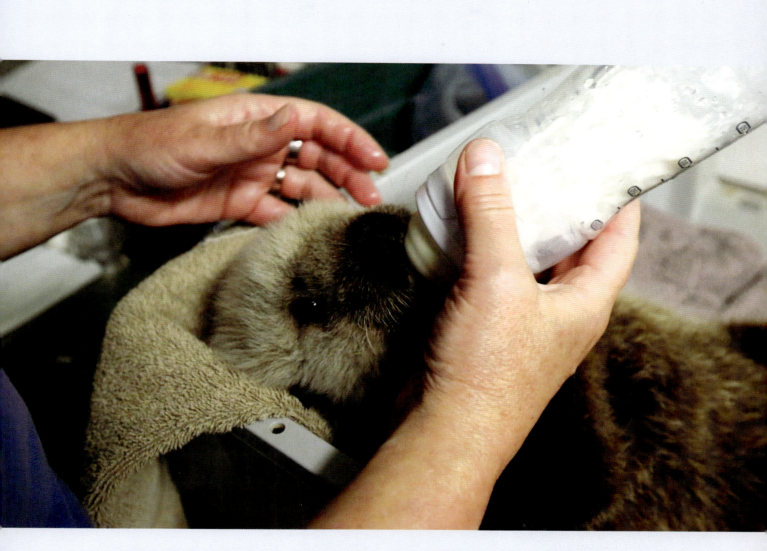

At the Seattle Aquarium, Rialto was nursed back to health with loving care around the clock.

Like most babies, Rialto slept a lot—as much as sixteen hours out of twenty-four. When he was rescued, he was just one to two weeks old and a little over a foot long, while adult otters can be five times that long. He still had so very much growing up to do! And he needed to get healthy. He had little muscle and no fat. He was just skin and bones. He had an upset stomach. And he had pneumonia, an infection in his lungs.

Rialto was given his own crib with a water-filled mattress to help him feel at home, as if he were floating on the sea. And he always had some ice cubes piled up in a bag for a pillow. Rialto liked the cold. Perhaps that was what it had felt like to rest against his mother's chest in the cold Pacific Ocean.

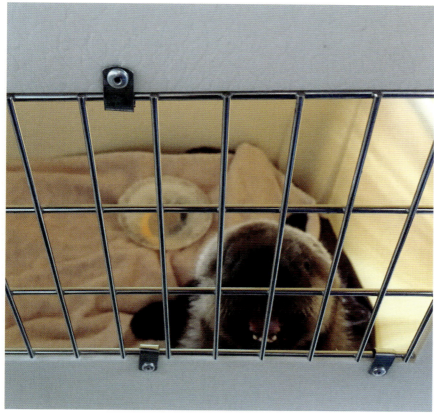

**Opposite page:** Rialto loved sleeping with a plastic bag full of ice cubes for a pillow.

**Top:** Rialto's caregivers made sure he always had new toys and plenty of ice cubes to chew on.

**Bottom:** Rialto had lots of favorite toys, and he was very clear about his needs. He shrieked whenever he wanted something.

Unlike seals and whales, sea otters don't have blubber, a thick layer of fat under the skin that keeps the animal warm in the cold ocean water. Instead, sea otters have the thickest fur coat of any animal on Earth: more than a half million hairs per square inch. It's so thick that, unlike human hair, you can't see the skin underneath when you part it.

Sea otter fur has two layers: a covering of long hairs called guard hairs and a very soft, dense layer underneath. Each hair has scales that interlock with one another, creating a jacket that traps air bubbles close to the otter's skin for insulation. Oil glands in their skin make their fur even more water-repellent. A healthy sea otter is warm, and waterproof!

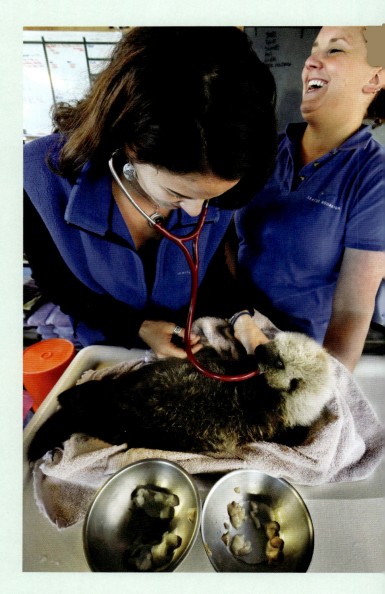

Rialto had a checkup shortly after he arrived at the Seattle Aquarium. He quickly got over his pneumonia and upset stomach and started fattening up.

Baby sea otters like Rialto have fur even fluffier than adults. It helps them float instead of sink, just like the life jacket you wear when you're on a boat. A baby sea otter's fur is a soft golden color. When the otter gets older, it grows the deep, rich brown fur of adults.

At first, Rialto stayed in a tiny room at the aquarium so Shawn and his other caretakers could keep a close eye on him. But within weeks, Rialto was getting better. He started gaining weight, and X-rays showed his lungs were clear. He was over the pneumonia.

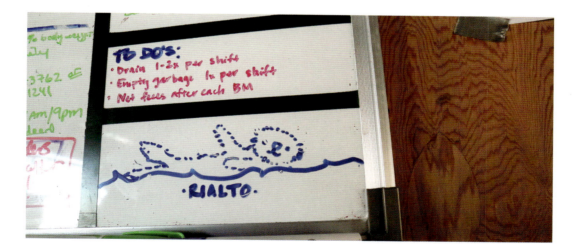

One of Rialto's caregivers added an artistic touch to the whiteboard the aquarium's staff used to track his daily progress. Not a bad likeness!

**Top:** Rialto always had lots to say. He would squeak to let his caregivers know he was enjoying his swim. **Bottom:** Rialto needed a little help to learn how to float on his back, but he quickly got the hang of it.

One day in early September, Shawn popped Rialto into a carrier like one you would use for a cat. It was time to move him to a place that would be more fun. He was well enough for his first swim.

Shawn carried Rialto up some steps, went around a corner, climbed some more steps, then opened the door of his carrier to let him enter a big outdoor cage. Even better, there was a pool.

Rialto knew just what to do. *Plop! Splash!* He could see daylight and hear the seagulls. His pool was full of water pumped in from Puget Sound, cold and salty, just the way he liked it. At first, he didn't know how to roll over onto his back and float, and Shawn had to support him with her hands. But soon he was steering with his thick, furry tail and thrusting with his fuzzy, webbed back feet to make turns. He nuzzled the fresh seawater.

Rialto made fast progress, quickly getting over his illness and moving to an outdoor cage with his very own pool.

Just a month after he was rescued, Rialto was swimming laps, sticking his head underwater, and blowing bubbles.

Whenever Rialto was ready to get out of his pool, he would put his paws up on the edge and shake his head just like a dog, sending silvery drops of water flying in all directions. Shawn laughed at that. She would reach in, pick Rialto up, and put him on her lap to dry him off with clean, soft towels. The staff at the aquarium did a lot of laundry for Rialto.

**Opposite page:** Time to get out after another nice long swim. Rialto's pool was filled with real salt water that was constantly circulated from Puget Sound.

**This page:** Drying off after a swim was a lot of work for both Rialto and Shawn Larson, requiring much headshaking on Rialto's part and many dry towels on Shawn's.

At around the same time that Rialto took his first swim, Shawn gave him his first taste of solid food: fresh, raw clam. Now, *that* was delicious. Rialto nibbled the clam right from her fingers. Then he wanted more and more.

Once Rialto started getting solid food, he couldn't get enough. Sometimes Shawn would feed him as he swam in his pool, leaving a bite-size piece of clam at the edge for him to snack on. He began learning how to feed himself using his paws. Shawn fed him more and more things: raw clams, shrimps, and squids. His teeth were starting to come in, too. An adult sea otter's front teeth are sharp and strong enough to bite right through the hard shell on a crab's claws. Otters also have flat molars in the backs of their mouths, just like humans do, for crushing food.

At first Rialto was hand-fed, but he soon learned how to feed himself using his paws.

**Top:** Rialto sizes up a tasty snack placed right where he can reach it.
**Bottom:** Rialto's baby teeth were quite impressive.

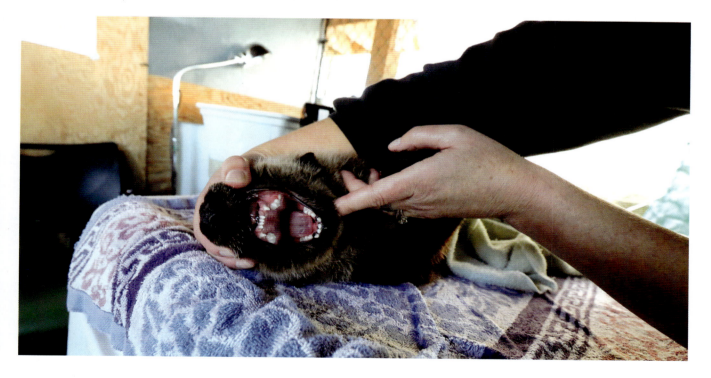

Rialto always had a fresh pile of ice cubes in a plastic bag for a pillow. His caregivers at the aquarium made him toys out of ice that had been frozen into fun shapes. Rialto often held on to his ice toy as he napped, gripping it with his front paws to avoid dropping it when he turned over. He used his claws, which are retractable like a cat's, to really grip things when he wanted to.

Rialto also had a ball to play with, and long pieces of felt like the kelp his mother had wrapped around him when he lived in the sea.

Rialto was getting bigger and stronger. He was becoming more and more lively and curious, investigating everything in his pool, diving, twirling, and chasing his tail for fun.

He was learning how to groom himself using his tongue and front paws, too. He learned how to put his head underwater and blow air into his fur to keep it fluffed up. In the wild, sea otters spend hours each day taking care of their coats to keep themselves warm and dry, even in extremely cold water.

Rialto tests out his baby teeth on a favorite toy. He spent lots of time swimming around on his back, paddling with his flipper-like hind paws.

**Top:** Strips of felt floating in the pool were meant to remind Rialto of the long, waving blades of green kelp in the wild.

**Bottom:** Rialto's caregivers used a blow-dryer to get him dry and fluffy.

Rialto had changed from a struggling, sick orphan into The Otter Who Would Not Be Ignored. If Rialto wanted to get back in his pool for a swim, he shrieked! If he wanted another ice toy, he shrieked! Or more clams? He shrieked and shrieked.

In the wild, sea otters live in large groups called rafts. They are homebodies, never straying far from the raft.

The aquarium staff gave him what he wanted right away, and even once he was healthy and strong, they never left him alone. Sea otters are very social. They mostly live together in large groups called rafts. They even link their front paws to stay together when they sleep, rest, or feed, the way people hold hands. That keeps them from getting separated by big waves. They stay close together, winding themselves in kelp so they don't drift off into the open sea, and they rarely range far from their home territory. Sea otter neighborhoods stick together for decades if there is enough food. The females and young stay in one raft, and the adult males in another.

Sea otters live out their lives less than a mile and a half from the shore. Near the shore is where they can harvest a wide variety of foods: scallops, mussels, snails, squids, crabs, clams, shrimps, and even octopuses, to name a few. And it's also where they can find one of their very favorite things of all: sea urchins.

A sea otter mother sometimes wraps her baby in kelp to keep it from drifting away while she dives for food.

Sea otters need to eat a lot, so they spend up to a third of their day hunting for food and eating.

Sea otters have to eat and eat to keep their body temperatures up in the cold ocean water. They spend about a quarter to a third of their day hunting for food and eating, and they need to eat about a quarter of their body weight every single day just to stay warm and active.

To get their meals, sea otters dive and gather food from the sea floor, using the sensitive pads of their front paws to feel for things they can't see. They tuck what they gather into pocket-like skin flaps under their front legs. Sometimes an otter will also pick up a rock before it swims back up to the surface. Then, when it's floating on its back, it lays the rock on its chest and swiftly hits clams and other shellfish on the rock over and over again to crack them open. Sea otters are one of the few species in the world that use tools to eat.

Rialto was growing fast, and his fur was slowly changing to the smoother, darker brown of an adult. But he still had a long way to go before he would reach his adult size of seventy to ninety pounds. That was a lot bigger than he was then, but sea otters are the smallest marine mammal. They are much smaller than seals, dolphins, sea lions, and killer whales. Sea otters are closer in size to their nearest animal relations, which include river otters, beavers, skunks, weasels, badgers, wolverines, and minks.

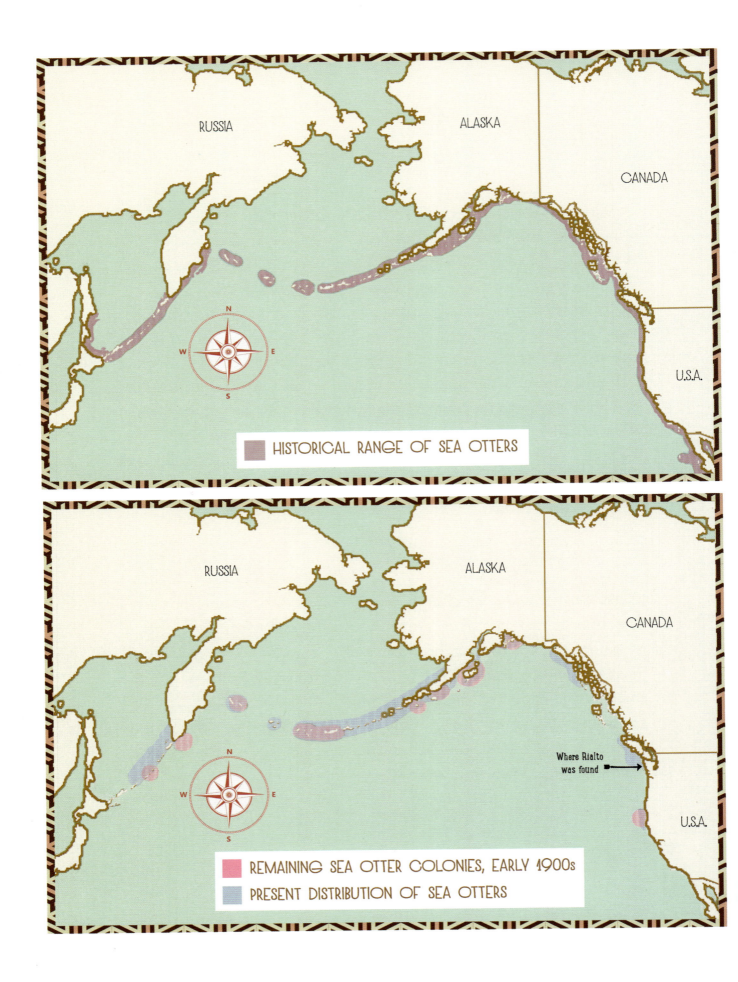

RUSSIA

ALASKA

CANADA

U.S.A.

HISTORICAL RANGE OF SEA OTTERS

RUSSIA

ALASKA

CANADA

Where Rialto
was found

U.S.A.

REMAINING SEA OTTER COLONIES, EARLY 1900s

PRESENT DISTRIBUTION OF SEA OTTERS

In August and September, Rialto had lots of visits from the staff at the aquarium in Vancouver, Canada, the nearest big city to Seattle. They were helping to take care of Rialto, and were also thinking about adopting him for their exhibit. The Vancouver Aquarium had a much bigger pool with room for a growing youngster. There, Rialto would be the only sea otter from Washington state for people in Vancouver to see.

Once, there were sea otters all along the Pacific coasts of Russia, Japan, and North America from Alaska all the way to Washington, Oregon, California, and Baja Mexico. Sea otters had been in those waters for about three million years.

Native people in all those places had coexisted with sea otters. Middens—the garbage dumps of people who lived long ago, found buried where they lived—include the bones of the animals the people hunted. At what was once an ancient native village in Washington, archaeologists found a bone from a sea otter's back that had a harpoon point thrust through it. This tells us that native people from thousands of years ago hunted sea otters for food.

We also know that they made robes from sea otters' warm, thick fur, and used their teeth to decorate ceremonial canoes, paddles, wooden chests, and other fine possessions.

Then came more hunters who wanted sea otters for their beautiful fur coats. First Russians came from the west, and then traders and explorers in North America arrived from the east. From 1741 until 1911, they killed sea otters in huge numbers for their coats, which they called pelts. Great piles of pelts were sent all the way to China on ships. The sea otter furs were sold there for a very high price.

Sea otters' natural range (top) included the coastlines of Russia, Japan, and North America, but hunting so diminished their numbers that by 1900, only a few pockets remained. Bottom: Efforts made over the past fifty years are slowly restoring the species to its original habitat.

Finally, in 1911, after the last sea otter in Washington was shot, a law was passed to protect them. It was almost too late. From 1911 to 1969, there were no sea otters along the coast of Washington.

Then, suddenly, there was no kelp, either. With no sea otters left to eat the sea urchins, there were too many urchins, and they ate all the kelp. Urchins love kelp. They mow it right down. Soon there were just bare rocks and sand. Without the great, swaying underwater forests of green kelp, tiny fish and other sea animals that had lived there no longer had homes. These bare places are called *urchin barrens*.

The whole nearshore environment had changed because the sea otters were gone. That is why sea otters are called a *keystone species*. Like the keystone at the top of an arch, they hold everything in their ecosystem together. A keystone species makes a place complete in terms of which plants and animals live there, and even what foods are available and how a place functions.

In 1969 and 1970, scientists decided to see if they could bring sea otters back. Although there were no more sea otters in Washington, some had survived in parts of Alaska. Scientists gathered up seventy-nine of them on Amchitka Island, Alaska, brought them to Washington's coast, and set them loose. They hoped these sea otters would make a new home in Washington. Not all the sea otters that were moved to Washington survived, but some did, and they had families. Today, all of the sea otters in Washington are related to those relocated animals from Alaska. Even Rialto!

More sea otters were moved to other sites in Alaska and British Columbia. When those sea otters went hunting in their new homes, they found all the sea urchins that had been multiplying while there were no sea otters around. The sea otters ate urchin after urchin. After the sea otters returned, the kelp grew back, once again swaying lush and green in the current, providing homes for small, darting fish such as juvenile salmon and rockfish, for crab larvae, and for other tiny sea creatures.

Sea urchins are among sea otters' very favorite foods. The prickly spines don't bother them one bit.

Today, sea otters dive through the beautiful kelp forests and drift in rafts above them just like before, their babies right alongside them. After being hunted nearly to extinction, there are now more than a hundred thousand wild sea otters living along the western coast of North America.

Yet it is still a rare treat for people to see a wild sea otter. Many have only seen them at aquariums. At the Vancouver Aquarium, they really wanted to have another baby sea otter for visitors to enjoy and learn from.

Just six weeks after Rialto first arrived in Seattle, Shawn got him up early and let him swim and swim and swim. She hoped he would get tired out: It was moving day. She fed him lots and lots of clams and lots and lots of shrimps. Then she got him dried off and comfortable. She held him tightly, and Rialto put one paw on her face.

Rialto seemed to know that Shawn Larson, his primary caregiver at the Seattle Aquarium, was saying goodbye as she dried him after his last swim in Seattle.

Sea otters have sensitive pads on their paws like cats do, and they use them to feel things, whether it is a clam on the bottom of the sea or, for Rialto, Shawn's face. It was as if he were saying, "It's okay, you can come visit!"

Soon it was time for Rialto to go. People arrived with a big carrier on wheels, and in he went. Shawn hurried alongside so he wouldn't be frightened. As the driver got behind the wheel, Shawn sat down in the back of the van, right next to Rialto in his carrier, holding his paw to keep him company. They were headed to Vancouver. "Eeeee!" shrieked Rialto. "Eeeee! Eeeee!"

Kristi Heffron, Rialto's head caregiver in Vancouver, had driven down to pick up Rialto, and to help keep him company, too. At the Canadian border, the guards asked if she or Shawn had anything to declare. "Just a sea otter," said Kristi.

"Eeeee!" said Rialto. His voice was so loud that people in cars nearby could hear him, even with all the van's doors and windows closed. "Eeeee!"

**Top:** There was time for a little after-swim nap before Rialto had to get in the crate for his big move from Seattle to the Vancouver Aquarium.

**Bottom:** Kristi Heffron of the Vancouver Aquarium watches Rialto have a nice, big stretch.

At the Vancouver Aquarium, the staff were waiting for him in the driveway. But they heard him before they saw him, of course. "Eeeee! Eeeee!" They wheeled Rialto on a cart to his new nursery and opened his cage. Rialto went straight for his pool and in for a swim. It seemed like anywhere there was water, Rialto felt at home.

Rialto's new caregivers gave him ice toys, and Shawn had brought his favorite foods and his bottle. There was a crib for him, one with high sides so he wouldn't tumble out, along with lots of fresh white towels to keep him dry and clean and fluffy.

In Vancouver, there were many, many people to take care of him, just like there had been in Seattle. So even though Shawn didn't want to leave Rialto, she knew it was time for her to go. She left, promising to come back soon.

In late October, a little more than a month after Rialto moved to Canada, Shawn came to visit him. She wondered, *Will Rialto know who I am?* "Hi, Muffin," she said as she came up to his crib. "Eeeee!" Rialto said. He knew who she was, all right.

Shawn let Rialto smell her hand, then gave him a big bucket of ice to play with. What fun he had, making the cubes fly! It was hard for Shawn to say goodbye when it was time to go.

**Opposite page, top:** When Rialto arrived in Vancouver, the aquarium staff rushed him from the van to his new home. **Bottom:** Rialto takes his first swim as staff members enjoy the newest arrival at the Vancouver Aquarium.

On November 1, Rialto had a new visitor. It was a woman with a carrier like the one Rialto had arrived in, and she brought it over to the big pool next to Rialto's nursery.

The visitor and Kristi opened the carrier door, and what should come out but two baby sea otters! They had been rescued, like Rialto. Named Mak and Kunik, these babies were from Alaska. They were just a little older than Rialto.

At first, Rialto stuck close to Kristi's feet as he watched Mak and Kunik tumble and play. Pretty soon, they came right up to Rialto and gave him a good looking over. After that, it wasn't long before Rialto hopped in the water, too.

Now, day after day, the three baby sea otters play and play. Silvery air bubbles trail from their coats as they dive in their ten thousand—gallon tank of seawater.

The babies' caregivers bring them fresh clams and fish to eat. At feeding time, the pups sit in the particular order they've been taught to: first, second, and third. They sleep in one big, wriggling, brown, furry pile atop a mound of ice cubes. And they dip and swirl and swim for hour after hour.

**Opposite page:** Luckily for Rialto, new friends soon joined him—baby sea otters Mak and Kunik from Alaska. What a threesome they make!

**Top:** Kristi Heffron points to where she wants Rialto to hop up onto the ledge to get ready for lunch. The ice scattered on the deck is for playing with.

**Bottom:** Rialto loves to have clam strips hand-fed to him as a treat.

Independent now, Rialto knows from just a hand signal to haul himself out of the pool to get fed. He swims all he wants, zooming around with Mak and Kunik. He's not in the wild, but for people visiting from all over the world, Rialto *is* an ambassador for Washington's wild sea otters.

Sometimes he seems to know it, sitting up extra tall, showing off just a little. Shawn noticed that he always pays special attention to the children who visit him at the Vancouver Aquarium, swimming right over to see them through the glass sides of his pool.

"He is just so sunny and brimming with joy and life," she said. "And being an otter."

**Opposite page:**
The only Washington sea otter at the Vancouver Aquarium, Rialto seems to know he is special as he swishes around in his tank, making swirls of bubbles.

**Top:** Rialto is great at diving deep in his new tank at the Vancouver Aquarium.

**Bottom:** Of all his visitors, Rialto seems to particularly enjoy the children. Here he is, looking at you!

## WHAT TO DO IF YOU FIND A STRANDED SEA OTTER OR OTHER MARINE MAMMAL

Do not touch it or pick it up; doing so is illegal under the Marine Mammal Protection Act. Wild animal rescue requires specialized care that is given by trained experts and must be authorized by government agencies on a case-by-case basis. It is never an easy decision—or always the right one—to rescue an animal.

Contact the wildlife agency or marine mammal stranding network in your community for help. You may stand watch over the animal to keep onlookers and dogs away, but don't get too close—your presence could scare the animal's mother away. Stay quiet, and do not bother or try to assist the animal in any way.

### SOURCES

Lance, Monique M., Scott A. Richardson, and Harriet L. Allen. *Washington State Recovery Plan for the Sea Otter*. Olympia, WA: Wildlife Program, Washington Department of Fish and Wildlife, December 2004. wdfw.wa.gov/publications/00314/wdfw00314.pdf.

Larson, Shawn E., James L. Bodkin, and Glenn R. VanBlaricom, editors. *Sea Otter Conservation*. London: Academic Press, 2015.

McNulty, Tim. "Washington's Otter Comeback." *Defenders*, Summer 1998. defenders.org/sites/default /files/publications/washingtons_otter_comeback.pdf.

Meeker, Clare Hodgson. *Lootas, Little Wave Eater: An Orphaned Sea Otter's Story*. Seattle: Sasquatch Books, 1999.

Washington Department of Fish and Wildlife. "Sea Otter (*Enhydra lutris*)." In *Threatened and Endangered Wildlife in Washington: 2012 Annual Report*. Olympia, WA: Listing and Recovery Section, Wildlife Program, Washington Department of Fish and Wildlife, 2013. pp. 37–9. wdfw.wa.gov/publications/01542 /wdfw01542.pdf.

### ACKNOWLEDGMENTS

Special thanks to the Seattle Aquarium, without which we would not have had access to this story of Rialto's rescue and recovery. Tim Kuniholm, Shawn Larson, and Traci Belting were wonderfully helpful and a joy to work with. At the Vancouver Aquarium, Deana Lancaster and Kristi Heffron have our thanks.
This book is based on our reporting for *The Seattle Times* in August, September, and December of 2016. At the *Times*, we thank our editors and colleagues for helping us tell this story.
Thanks also to our editor at Macmillan, Simon Boughton, who reached out to suggest creating this book.